TECHNIC

Heart of Darkness

*Prepared by Cicely Havely
for the Course Team*

The Open University Press

The Open University Press
Walton Hall Milton Keynes

First published 1973.

Designed by the Media Development Group of the Open University.

Printed in Great Britain by
Martin Cadbury, a specialised division of Santype International, Worcester and London

ISBN 0 335 00827 5

This text forms part of an Open University course. The complete list of units in the course is given at the end of this text.

For general availability of supporting material referred to in this text, please write to the Director of Marketing, The Open University, P. O. Box 81, Walton Hall, Milton Keynes, MK7 6AA.

Further information on Open University courses may be obtained from the Admissions Office, The Open University, P.O. Box 48, Walton Hall, Milton Keynes, MK7 6AA.

1.1

CONTENTS

Introductory Note

In both Sections your main task will be to relate *Heart of Darkness* to earlier novels on the Course, and identify some of the significant developments it represents. The Unit does contain more guidance towards understanding the novel for its own sake than this approach absolutely necessitates, but you will find it mixed with, or following, the general discussions which are our main concern, and not set out on its own.

Acknowledgements

The author wishes to thank Arnold Kettle, Graham Martin, Nick Furbank, Dennis Johnson and Helen Rapp for their help and advice.

Joseph Conrad c. *1911 (Photo: E. O. Hoppe. Mansell Collection)*

NOTES ON UNITS 27–32

onrad began writing *Heart of Darkness* in 1898, only three years after the publication of *Jude the Obscure*. The division between 'nineteenth-' and 'twentieth-century' fiction is naturally arbitrary and in various ways unsatisfactory. You can argue plausibly that by 1895 'Victorian England' was already well on the way out (certainly *Jude* presses most insistently into our own century) or, alternatively, that 1914 is the vital date if one wants to mark the ending of an era. Fair enough. We aren't trying, in this Course, to test out historical generalizations with any sort of rigour, or to nail our colours to one particular year, or even decade, as ending the period we've thought of as 'nineteenth-century'. If we make a distinction between nineteenth- and twentieth-century fiction it's in full knowledge that it's a distinction open to all kinds of legitimate reservations.

Yet there can hardly be any doubt, if you think about the novels of Conrad, of Forster, of Lawrence and Joyce and Virginia Woolf, that something has happened: a new fiction is making itself felt. Not that anyone would claim that the five writers are much alike. Forster is, pretty clearly, the least interested in making innovations: Joyce perhaps the most experimental. We aren't concerned, in these next few units, to try to define exhaustively, much less to explain, the 'new spirit' (sometimes referred to as 'modernism') in the early twentieth-century novel—a spirit which, incidentally, was by no means confined to Britain. The names of Proust and Gide, Kafka and Mann, are relevant too. *But this is not a history of the novel nor a thorough-going examination of the new novel.* We are, unashamedly, using these five novelists for our own particular purposes: *to help us to look back on the nineteenth-century novel and decide what, as a general literary phenomenon, it was like.*

'What do they know of England' Kipling was saying at just this moment, at the turn of the century, 'who only England know?' Precisely. How can you get a phenomenon into any kind of perspective without acquiring some sense of what it grows out of and leads into? How to sum up an achievement in a vacuum? We only know what we are doing when we've done it.

The Course Team is well aware of the dangers of 'using' a body of literature, even with the best intentions. But we're not, it must be emphasized, out to make high new claims or to force tricky critical issues. Our objects are, rather:

(i) to help you to an adequate reading of each of the twentieth-century pieces you are faced with, noting its particular quality and flavour;

(ii) to draw special attention, in these new fictions, to the ways in which they seem to
(a) develop from
(b) break away from
the 'norms' of the nineteenth-century novel;

(iii) to try to define (or perhaps re-define), in the light of these considerations, the most important characteristics of the nineteenth-century novels we have been studying, trying to see them now as constituting a coherent body of literature.

It's true of course that the use of the word 'norms' (even in inverted commas) in the second objective assumes that you have already reached some tentative conclusions about the 'coherence' of the novels you have been studying. That is why I speak of 're-defining' as the third objective. We hope that Units 27–31 will help you to take a fruitful, new look at the more general conclusions that have already begun to emerge from your work on Units 1–26.

The Units that follow aren't uniform in their structure or emphasis. Each writer is discussed in the ways which seem most appropriate to the author of the unit. If we stress the methodologizing aims and objectives of this part of the Course it isn't because we wish to make inordinate claims for it, but rather that we are anxious to avoid disappointing students who are seeking a fuller or different kind of treatment of our authors from the one implicit in Units 27–31. That, to quote Kipling again, would be another story.

Arnold Kettle

1 NARRATIVE TECHNIQUE

As you work through this Unit, make notes under brief headings of everything you notice that is new about this novel, compared with those we have so far studied. You may well notice more new features than are discussed here. At the end of the Unit you will find a brief summing up which you should compare with your own notes, and keep by you for reference when you come to read the four other short novels which conclude this Course.

Many of the aspects which seem new will, as you think about them, turn out to have some kind of precedent. Often, the distinction will be a quantitative one: *Heart of Darkness* has *more* of certain qualities than earlier novels, rather than qualities which are entirely new. As you work, you should think about what this implies.

And if *Heart of Darkness* has more of some things than earlier novels, it seems likely that it will have less of others. What do you not find in this novel that you have found abundantly in other novels? And do you miss these things? You'll find my comments on p. 33.

Now read *Heart of Darkness*, and then the relevant sections of Franklin Walker's brief Introduction.[1]

You may have thought that instruction a bit terse. I didn't say 'Now read *Heart of Darkness* carefully, paying particular attention to . . . etc.' But you probably realized before you reached the bottom of the first page that there is only one possible way of reading this novel: that is, extremely carefully. Some novels are so easy to read that the temptation is to rush through them, promising yourself all the time that you will immediately go back for a second, more attentive reading. Throughout this Course we've tried to persuade you that a scanty first reading isn't advisable; with this novel it's barely possible. Rush through it and you'll get nothing out of it. Rather like *What Maisie Knew* it demands your concentrated attention all the time: miss a phrase or a word and you may go wrong. And again like James's novel, in a sense all the difficulty is curiously near the surface. There are some novels (on our Course *Anna Karenina* is probably the best example) where complexity and problems are almost the last things you notice. There are others, like *What Maisie Knew* and *Heart of Darkness* where they are the first. This doesn't necessarily mean that they will be problematic all the way through. I don't mean that these novels are like

---

[1] The edition referred to throughout is the edition in Bantam Critical Editions, edited by Franklin Walker, 1969.

badly made jam—all the fruit at the top, and half the jar just thin syrup. These novels are rich through and through, but a barrier of difficulty has to be crossed before you can get to the heart of the matter. Let me put it another way: you may have found with both these novels that you can't proceed to discuss broad issues as quickly or easily as you can with some other novels. It takes longer to get on easy terms with them.

Perhaps you have already noticed that I call this work a novel, and not a 'long short story' or a 'novella'. It's largely a matter of taste: I rejected the former because it's cumbersome, faintly ridiculous, and begs a lot of questions; and the latter because, deservedly or not, it sounds much too frivolous for *Heart of Darkness*. The label we use doesn't matter much, but the fact that we could assemble five short novels of this quality from this period and *without difficulty* is highly significant. Most of the nineteenth-century novelists studied earlier in this Course wrote shorter works: George Eliot's first published fiction was *Scenes from Clerical Life*, Dickens' most famous short work is *A Christmas Carol*. But the great authors of the nineteenth century could not as a whole be fairly represented by their shorter works. Towards the end of the century however, more and more shorter works of the highest quality began to emerge: Henry James *can* be fairly represented by *What Maisie Knew*, which, although it may have taken you as long to read as *Great Expectations*, is, in number of words, considerably shorter than any earlier novel on this Course, and shorter than many of James's own major works.

Can you think of any reason for this relatively sudden increase in the number of first class short novels?

Some portion of the cause must be attributed to changes in publishing methods. These will be discussed in Unit 32, but for the moment it is enough to note that the novelist was no longer obliged by his publishers to fill three large volumes; what length he chose was up to the writer himself.

Another answer might seem to be that the novelist was adapting his product to his market: shorter novels for busier people. But this doesn't get us far because some of these shorter novels demand proportionately far harder work. Neither *What Maisie Knew* nor *Heart of Darkness* was designed for bed-time reading. (And in any case the leisured middle class still had plenty of time on its hands.) But the novel-reading public *had* changed (see Unit 23 Section 2, *The Good and the Popular*), and writers like Conrad recognized this. They were writing for the intelligent, discriminating minority. Naturally they wanted their readership to be as large as possible, but they would not cut back their own high standards, nor restrain their wish to see how far and in what new directions the novel could be taken.

The real answer must be that novelists were trying to do different things, deliberately breaking away from the forms and assumptions of the nineteenth-century novel. Henry James was not so much the cause, as the most dramatic symptom of a great upheaval in the development of the novel. *Jude the Obscure*, almost contemporaneous with *What Maisie Knew*, is not only about the struggles of its central characters. Hardy was challenging old gods and old standards and in a very real sense his novel is also about the struggles of the novelist to obtain a new role and a new freedom, as well as new responsibilities. James was the major spokesman for the novel's great leap forwards, but he wasn't the sole impulse behind it. He recognized that the 'loose baggy monsters' had evolved as far as they could, and from about this time they were dead as mastodons.

(Popular novels, on the other hand, were looser and baggier than ever: a good example is Galsworthy's *Forsyte Saga*.) You will remember from Units 16–17 that James stressed the importance of the art of the novel: it must be well made, and the novelist as sensitive to his creation and as deliberative as any other kind of artist. I hope you were struck by Conrad's deliberation. Perhaps you felt unsure about what he was trying to do: most people have similar difficulties, and we'll look at why this should be so later. But I hope you would agree that from the beginning of this novel it is clear that Conrad has set himself an intellectual and artistic task, and then tried to complete it.

This course is called *The Nineteenth-Century Novel and its Legacy*. Conrad's novel has obvious differences from anything we have read before, but is there anything about it that connects it with the novels we have so far studied? What of his inheritance has Conrad chosen to use?

This is not a question I want to answer all at once, but I imagine that one thing in particular may have struck you: the prominent role of the narrator. This has been an issue that we have returned to over and over again in this Course. Before reading on, pause and make a few general notes on Marlow's role in this novel. You will find it useful to read the relevant extract from Jocelyn Baines's biography, printed on pages 205–11 of your edition.

I expect that the first question you asked yourself was: Is Marlow Conrad? Obviously to a certain extent he is, but whether or not Conrad had his Mr Kurtz remains in doubt: we know nothing of Klein beyond the fact that he died while Conrad was taking him back down-river. But whether or not a man like Kurtz was a prominent part of Conrad's nightmare on the Congo, nightmare it certainly seems to have been. But Conrad's reaction, as far as we know it, had less mystery about it than Marlow's. In *Geography and Some Explorers* (one of his last essays) he describes his feelings when he first set foot on the spot which had so fascinated him as a boy: he was not thrilled, but felt

only the unholy recollection of a prosaic newspaper 'stunt' and the distasteful knowledge of the vilest scramble for loot that ever disfigured the history of human conscience and geographical exploration.

(The 'stunt' was Henry Morton Stanley's expedition to find Emin Pasha. Conrad had a life-long hatred of journalists.) It seems to have been the spoliation of the Congo that particularly affected him. Elsewhere, he describes *Heart of Darkness* as 'all the spoil I brought from out the centre of Africa, where, really, I had no business'. Conrad and Marlow certainly share a profound disgust for the hideous malpractices of the colonizers. Whether they share an apprehension of anything more arcane than ordinary, sordid human greed, we cannot know.

To a certain extent Marlow is Conrad. So who, then, is the other first person narrator in *Heart of Darkness*?

Perhaps you didn't even notice him. In any case, read the first two pages again, and make notes on his role.

The first person singular is used only once here. ('Between us there was, as I have already said somewhere, the bond of the sea') and only very sparingly hereafter. Mostly the first person *plural* is used: 'The Director of companies was our captain and our host. We four . . . etc.' 'We four' are the Lawyer, the Accountant, Marlow, and the narrator. Of the five men altogether three are known only by their professions—curiously safe, respectable, land-lubbing occupations in spite of the Director's appearance. The narrator is entirely anonymous. I'm not going to spend any time worrying about the significance of the Company Director, the Lawyer and the Accountant. I'm sure you have already allotted them as much significance as they need: any more you can leave to those who can find nothing better to do with the novel.

Most of the time we forget the first person narrator, and even at the beginning and end of the novel he is only a very insubstantial presence. Surely Conrad did not introduce a narrator like this to make a great mystery out of him, so what do you think he's doing in the story?

He's only the 'author' in a very minimal sense. The story and it's interpretations are Marlow's. The person I want to call the 'outermost narrator' is a sort of secretary, an official recorder, who takes down Marlow's story, and passes it on. The story hardly needs him, but clearly (or why else include him?) Conrad did. The outermost narrator's part is so small that his real importance seems to me to be that of a private reminder to Conrad to keep Marlow at a distance, to objectify him, and to remember that whatever closeness there might be in the story to his own experience, nevertheless that experience must all stand up and be judged as if by someone completely impartial and remote from it. So a first person narrator is introduced, and given something more like the reader's part than the writer's. At the same time, he offers the reader some kind of guidance about how to interpret Marlow's barely defined, mysterious, subjective account of his experiences. He tells us plainly enough what we are in for—'. . . we knew we were fated, before the ebb began to run, to hear about one of Marlow's inconclusive experiences' (p. 10).

He also tells us what aspects of his story Marlow is most interested in:

. . . to him the meaning of an episode was not inside like a kernel but outside, enveloping the tale which brought it out only as a glow brings out a haze, in the likeness of one of those misty halos that sometimes are made visible by the spectral illumination of moonshine.

(p. 7)

—is it only because it is such a clumsy sentence that it looks as much like a warning as a promise? As well as approximating to the reader's part, this narrator offers something like an author's preface.

It may be that the framework also gives an ironic hint of what Conrad expects his readers' reactions to be. Marlow's preamble 'was accepted in silence. No one took the trouble to grunt even' (p. 7). And for his immediate audience's reaction to his whole story, look at the final paragraph!

We could go on worrying at this much longer, and still not come to any conclusions. In these last Units of the Course, however, we don't need to bother over much about the conclusions we might reach about any particular novel: we are primarily concerned with more general issues. So here what I want to concentrate on is not any 'answer' there might be to this particular 'problem', but the fact that the 'problem' of the narrator, and related, inseparable issues like point of view and the author's place in his work are at least as prominent here as they have been throughout the Course. In many ways *Heart of Darkness* seems to be as unlike a 'typical' nineteenth-century novel as it can possibly be; and yet I think we can confidently maintain that a tradition does connect this novel with those we have studied earlier, if only on the evidence of this one relating factor alone. (Later, I shall want to go on to suggest that there are considerably more relating factors than this.) We've often looked at how these things work in a novel, and now is the time to try to pull together some of our findings.

First, in one way or another, the novelist is drawing attention to what he is doing, and asserting the validity of telling a story. To me it seems like a strange, long-lived survival of Romanticism. So much Romantic poetry is actually *about* writing poetry; so many nineteenth-century novels are in a sense about telling a story—or at very least, they draw attention to the fact that a story is being told, and is not telling itself. This is one more contribution the outermost narrator, who at first seems so insignificant, makes to *Heart of Darkness*. He is the person who re-tells Marlow's story to a wider audience than the Lawyer, the Accountant and the Company Director. Conrad's belief that his story is worth reading is thus given an identity and made prominent.

Let's pursue this a bit further by comparing *Heart of Darkness* with two earlier novels: *Wuthering Heights* and *Huckleberry Finn*. Can you see any obvious points of comparison between each of these and Conrad's novel?

You may have said that *Wuthering Heights* is at least partly about abnormal psychological states, and may be you felt vaguely that there is a kind of darkness at the heart of both novels—however, I don't propose to pursue that one any further. The most obvious feature that Twain's novel shares with Conrad's is that it's about a river journey. (You can make what you like of the fact that one journey goes up-, the other down-stream.) In both, the journey is richly symbolic. And in both, the story is told by the person who made the journey. (From now on, I am talking about the 'inner' story, and its narrator, Marlow.)

In their different ways both Huck and Marlow are conscious that the journey has been significant for *them*: look at the following passages:

It was fifteen minutes before I could work myself up to go and humble myself to a nigger—but I done it, and I warn't ever sorry for it afterwards, neither. I didn't do him no more mean tricks, and I wouldn't done that one if I'd a knowed it would make him feel that way.

Huckleberry Finn, p. 143

Now try for a moment to imagine Marlow's story told with the significance only apparent to Conrad and his readers. Take for instance one of the major themes of *Heart of Darkness*, the corruptness of colonial administration. Conrad could have written a novel in which this was perfectly apparent to the reader, but not to any of the characters in the novel. But Marlow and Huck are aware of at least part of the significance of the stories they figure in. What's more, their understanding seems to be increased by the act of telling. Each has been put in a position where he must tell his story, and telling it helps him to understand it. Again, this mirrors the novelist's function and experience. He understands his material better as he comes to grips with the problems of telling it. (And again, I think we can still see a parallel with the preoccupations of the Romantic poets by looking at the end of Coleridge's *Ancient Mariner*.)

Now if we apply this theorem to *Wuthering Heights* we can see something of the same principles at work. You'll remember that it has a very complex structure of narrative within narrative. The outermost narrative belongs to Mr Lockwood; he doesn't present the bulk of the story, which is told by Nelly Dean, but he is always present as a listener, and (although his role is more complex) he can thus be compared with Conrad's first person narrator. And both can be said to reflect the reader's part.

At this point you may find it useful to re-read quickly Unit 4, Section 1 on the narrative technique of *Wuthering Heights*. There, Graham Holderness stresses the 'ordinariness' of Lockwood and Nelly compared with the other characters of the novel, and suggests that they act as a kind of filter for the central action. But apart from his 'ordinariness' what kind of man is Lockwood at the beginning of the novel? And is he still the same kind of man at the end?

At the beginning he is undoubtedly a rather trivial character, and even at the end, from the few glimpses we have of him it's clear that Wuthering Heights is still like a foreign country to him, and his mannerisms and idiom remain self-conscious and stilted. But some 'sudden impulse' takes him back to the Heights, where he sees young Catherine, and Hareton, whom a year ago he had summed up as a 'clown' and a 'bore', and whom he had laughed at 'internally . . . [for] the dignity with which he announced himself'. Hareton has changed, of course, but surely so has Lockwood. He respects the boy's efforts to educate himself, and he is half in love with young Catherine. Of course, he doesn't want to join the world of Wuthering Heights, partly because it can't be joined: it belonged only to a few people, for a short space of time. But his new feelings show that he has learnt something from the story he has heard, which we can assess by looking at the last few paragraphs of the novel. Nelly tells him that Wuthering Heights is to be shut up:

'And who will live here then?'

'Why, Joseph will take care of the house, and, perhaps, a lad to keep him company. They will live in the kitchen, and the rest will be shut up.'

'For the use of such ghosts as choose to inhabit it,' I observed.

'No, Mr Lockwood,' said Nelly, shaking her head. 'I believe the dead are at peace, but it is not right to speak of them with levity.'

(p. 366)

You can judge how well Lockwood heeds Nelly's advice, and how far he has understood her whole story, by reading the very last paragraph of the novel.

On the evidence of *Wuthering Heights* and *Huckleberry Finn* then it would seem that various kinds of first person narrators were used so frequently by nineteenth-century novelists not just as a favoured technical device for engaging the reader's interest, but also because they could be useful in communicating the moral aspects of a novel. The earliest novelists felt a need to justify their products by insisting that they had a moral lesson to teach and, as we have seen, this tradition persisted throughout the nineteenth century in various subtly modified forms. The use of a first person narrator can demonstrate the lesson being learnt: another obvious example of this is *Great Expectations*.

To get back from the general to the more particular: I think there is one more point to be made by comparing *Heart of Darkness* with *Wuthering Heights*. Nelly's role corresponds roughly with Marlow's. It is not enough to say that she is simply an observer. She is engaged in the action: suffers with some of the characters, or because of them; judges and applauds; understands some of the things she sees and fails to understand others. She saw Heathcliff's arrival at the Heights, and she has survived him. But of course *Wuthering Heights* is not as much *about* Nelly as *Heart of Darkness* is *about* Marlow. Here, an obvious point of comparison is once again with *What Maisie Knew*. *Heart of Darkness* is a very portentous title, but a possible sub-title could well be What Marlow Knew— or at least What Marlow Found Out. He's practically as much of a blank as Maisie when he sets out, and whether he has really learnt anything more important than she discovered when he returns is a moot point.[1]

What marks these two novels off from earlier first person narratives, or novels written from the point of view of a single character is firstly the intensity of the author's scrutiny of his character's mental processes, secondly the fact that these processes form the major movement of the novels in question, and thirdly (and most important) the author's decision to stick as closely and as exclusively as he can to the point of view he has chosen, and not to allow himself easier, alternative points of view when the going gets tough. James and Conrad both set themselves hard rules of narrative procedure, and they stand by them through thick and thin.

We've seen that James and Conrad were both building on a tradition of narrative technique, but can you think of any contemporary impulse from outside the novelist's sphere which might have suggested to these two authors that the minutest workings of a character's mind were important, and deserved the fullest display?

Here we have to be vague. We cannot say that Conrad was influenced by Freud and the development of psycho-analysis, because Freud's theories were not available when *Heart of Darkness* was written. But we can say that psychiatrists were not the only group of people interested in the obscurer workings of the mind: artists too were beginning to analyse the subconscious urges and motivations of their subjects. (This is not just true of a complex novelist like Conrad; it is also to be found in a reputedly strightforward storyteller such as Kipling.)

Related to this is a tendency in the novelists of the early twentieth century to go for the deep, rather than the broad. I'm not suggesting that nineteenth-century novelists were not capable of profundity. It's more a distinction of form, and at this stage in our work on post nineteenth-century fiction it is not fair to expect you to see distinctions clearly. But compare the number of characters in *Heart of Darkness* with the number in any earlier novels. Only one (Marlow) is anything like a complete portrait, and he makes no claim to know the people he encounters very fully. Indeed, one of the things the story is about

---

[1] Is *Huckleberry Finn* more 'about' Huck than *Heart of Darkness* is 'about' Marlow?

is how impossible it is for him to understand Kurtz, in spite of knowing a considerable number of facts about him. Compare Pip in *Great Expectations*: there, once the 'facts' of Miss Havisham's, or Mr Jaggers's, or Magwitch's case have been discovered, the assumption is that they are understandable. The assumption in *Heart of Darkness* is that Marlow knows only himself—and not even himself very fully: everyone else must in varying degrees remain unknown.

We can go on from this to say that nineteenth-century novels were, by and large, about societies, whereas the early twentieth-century novels were more about individuals. (In this course, you could regard *What Maisie Knew* as the turning point.) Of course, this is not to say that George Eliot was not interested in individuals, nor Conrad in the workings of society. But the emphasis has shifted.

One of the elements responsible for this shift was surely the changing way in which the novelist viewed his own role. George Eliot and Dickens (though their attitudes were not identical) saw themselves as part of the society in which they lived. Conrad, Virginia Woolf and D. H. Lawrence, with varying degrees of consciousness, felt themselves to be distinct from the society in which the majority of their contemporaries lived. Their sense of separateness manifested itself in various ways. D. H. Lawrence came to hate what he saw as the mediocrity of standards and expectations in all sections of English society so much that he lived much of the last part of his life abroad. James Joyce had to leave Ireland to be able to see it clearly: he had to establish his separateness. Virginia Woolf and the Bloomsbury circle were often afflicted by a sense of their superiority. In his personal life, Conrad seems an exception: he was a Polish expatriate who greatly desired to be a thorough English gentleman—but perhaps the England he wanted to join only existed in his imagination. Almost all his novels contain examples of different kinds of extreme isolation, which he saw as a sort of disease of his times. It is a sign of something wrong in society that Kurtz can become isolated from his kind.

We cannot say that a novelist like Conrad was no longer concerned with society; but he was equally concerned with other things: with the separateness of the individual consciousness, and with himself as an artist. Conrad knew Henry James well, and the post-Jamesian care that has gone into the construction of *Heart of Darkness* is obvious. But I do want to elaborate certain comparisons that can be made between Conrad's methods and those of other kinds of artists. We can call them Conrad as poet, as painter, and as photographer—or perhaps camera-man, because the picture moves.

First, the poetry of this novel. You cannot have missed the density and compression of Conrad's language. Every word was deliberately chosen, and demands a very lively awareness of its operations; but just how much *more* deliberative than earlier novelists Conrad was in his choice of words, is a matter of degree, and in any case has little to do with anything akin to poetry that there might be about the presentation of this story. (You can find some of Conrad's own thoughts about his medium on pp. 319–21 of *Novelists on the Novel*.[1]) Nor is it poetic in the sense that it is beautiful. I don't really think it is—not just because Conrad was not a native English speaker, but partly because he chose to approximate to the plain-speaking voice of the not very poetic Charlie Marlow. *Heart of Darkness* is a poetic novel in that so much of its weight is carried by metaphors and symbols. As always, this is not entirely new. We looked at something very like symbolism in *Mansfield Park*. But in no novel we have so far studied do symbolism and metaphor carry the responsibility for so much.

[1] Miriam Allott, *Novelists on the Novel*, Routledge & Kegan Paul, 1959 (SET BOOK).

Colonists with bearer by the Congo River (Radio Times Hulton Picture Library)

Here they are in no sense an extra, or a luxury of ornament. They are essential to the fabric of the novel and carry an extremely large proportion of its significance. If you have not previously made notes on the use of symbols in this novel, look at the fog which prevents the steamer reaching Kurtz (p. 65 ff.), or the two women in the Company's office (p. 15 ff.).

It's possible that you felt rather overwhelmed by the extent of Conrad's use of symbolism. Every object seems to exude significance—even, for example, things as prosaic as the rivets seem to have a larger meaning:

. . . several times a week a coast caravan came in with trade goods—ghastly glazed calico that made you shudder only to look at it, glass beads value about a penny a quart, confounded spotted cotton handkerchiefs. And no rivets. Three carriers could have brought all that was wanted to set that steamboat afloat.

. . . what I wanted was a certain quantity of rivets—and rivets were what really Mr Kurtz wanted, if he had only known it.

(p. 46)

The rivets carry with them qualities of decency, practicality, solidity and down-to-earthness. Down at the coast they are scattered and squandered. Only after immense effort can they finally be brought into the madhouse of the Central Station. You may feel this is a disproportionate emphasis for things as insignificant as rivets: but in a world where reality is so elusive, solid things assume immense importance, and the normal degrees of significance no longer apply. In the Congo, a rivet may be the one thing necessary.

This is not to say that Conrad does not occasionally go too far. A test-case is Marlow's description of his visit to the Company's Head Office, on pages 15–16. It's a very esoteric passage, which demands that the reader know more than just an outline of classical mythology. The two women are related to the Fates (the Parcae or Moerae) and are conflated with Charon, who sits at the entrance to Hades, and ferries the dead across the river Styx. The Fates were spinners, hence the 'black wool as for a warm pall'. The Belgian women knit 'feverishly', perhaps, as a sign of the particular perils that lie in wait in the Congo. Clotho, the youngest of the Fates, presided over men's births: 'People were arriving, and the younger one was walking back and forth introducing them.' Lachesis, the second sister, was chance: 'The swift and indifferent placidity of that look troubled me. Two youths with foolish and cheery countenances were being piloted over, and she threw at them the same quick glance of unconcerned wisdom.' The third sister, Atropos, who cut the thread, is not there: Marlow is not to die in the Congo. Whatever you think of this passage, it is clear that none of the novels we have so far studied have demanded this kind of attention.

The most widespread symbolic usage in this novel is the continual use of the extremes of light and darkness, almost invariably placed side by side. This is established on the first page of the novel, where the sea and sky are luminous with the last of the light, whilst the city lies under 'a mournful gloom'. This and the following paragraphs might suggest that the metaphorical light is to be found only away from cities and land, in the freedom of the oceans—a point of view you might expect from a sailor. But is this all? Read on to the beginning of Marlow's story, at the top of page 10. Is the first equation, of darkness with the city, and light with the river going down to the sea, consistently followed?

When Marlow suddenly says 'And this also . . . has been one of the dark places of the earth' he is clearly prompted to his metaphorical remark by the deepening physical darkness, and this should give us a clue about what is to happen in the rest of the novel. The physical world is not cut to correspond with the metaphorical in any crude way. The effect of the sunset is described in broadly realistic terms, and its contrasts of light and shadow suggest another kind of contrast, which is not an exact parallel at all. London is dark, but is also 'the biggest, *and the greatest*, town on earth'. But how does he describe Brussels, which he obviously does not think much of?

'I arrived in a city that always makes me think of a whited sepulchre.' On the other hand, the Company's offices were in 'a narrow and deserted street *in deep shadow*'. There is no simple equation of light and good, darkness and evil. The physical world (and this goes for the Congo as well as the Thames) is presented in a broadly realistic way, but it holds vast enigmas: London is dark but splendid ('We live in the flicker—may it last as long as the old earth keeps rolling!' p. 7) whilst Brussels is a 'whited sepulchre'. The moral world is equally difficult to read. It continually throws up hints of light or darkness, but it is not always possible to tell which is which, and it is certainly not possible to establish an infallible correspondence between the clues from the physical world, and any moral identity it might have. The jungle, for example, is physically dark, but is it a place of complete moral darkness? For Marlow it was a place of enlightenment. Was it not also a place of enlightenment for Kurtz? But his light was obviously a kind of darkness. (Think of the white fog that seems to bar the approach to him.) Try to make up your mind whether this is simply playing with concepts, or whether Conrad is really wrestling with a serious philosophical problem. I shall come back to a related question at the very end of this Unit. If you need help here (and you certainly should not feel ashamed if you do), I include a few examples of Conrad's use of contrasts between light and darkness. If you feel quite confident that you recognize the extensiveness of Conrad's use of symbolic contrasts, simply read through. If you are at all confused, read *two or three* of these passages in their context, and make notes. How many of these passages are exclusively descriptive?

p. 40   Then I noticed a small sketch in oils, on a panel, representing a woman, draped and blindfolded, carrying a lighted torch. The background was sombre—almost black. The movement of the woman was stately, and the effect of the torchlight on the face was sinister.

p. 41   He blew the candle out suddenly, and we went outside. The moon had risen. Black figures strolled about listlessly, pouring water on the glow, whence proceeded a sound of hissing; steam ascended in the moon-light, the beaten nigger groaned somewhere.

p. 43   The smell of mud, of primeval mud, by Jove! was in my nostrils, the high stillness of primeval forest was before my eyes; there were shiny patches on the black creek. The moon had spread over everything a thin layer of silver—over the rank grass, over the mud, upon the wall of matted vegetation standing higher than the wall of a temple, over the great river I could see through a sombre gap glittering, glittering, as it flowed broadly by without a murmur.

p. 55   There was no joy in the brilliance of sunshine. The long stretches of the waterway ran on, deserted, into the gloom of over-shadowed distances. On silvery sand-banks hippos and alligators sunned them-selves side by side.

p. 62–3 . . . the back had been lovingly stitched afresh with white cotton thread, which looked clean yet . . . Not a very enthralling book; but at the first glance you could see there a singleness of intention, an honest concern for the right way of going to work, which made these humble pages, thought out so many years ago, luminous with another than a professional light.

p. 65   When the sun rose there was a white fog, very warm and clammy, and more blinding than the night.

p. 79   . . . his ability to talk, his words—the gift of expression, the bewildering, the illuminating, the most exalted and the most contemptible, the pulsating stream of light, or the deceitful flow from the heart of an impenetrable darkness.

p. 117   One evening coming in with a candle I was startled to hear him say a little tremulously, 'I am lying here in the dark waiting for death.' The light was within a foot of his eyes.

Unlike Henry James or later, Virginia Woolf, Conrad's art does not readily suggest comparisons with the art of the painter. But in this story at least he seems to have selected his range of colours with a painter's eye. I've said that his descriptions of the physical world are broadly realistic: it would be better

Bird's eye view of Stanley
Pool on the Congo River
(Radio Times Hulton
Picture Library)

to say that they are convincing. This jungle is not bright green, and replete
with parrots; the sun does not stand in a blue sky. The landscape is black and
white and silver—and, of course, ivory—with only the occasional flash of scarlet
or bronze. The physical world has been coloured to suit Conrad's moral
purposes.

You may not have felt that Conrad is a very visual novelist. He seems to expend
so much effort trying to see deep into things that he does not see them in the
ordinary sense at all. But look carefully at the following passage:

I was looking down at the sounding-pole, and feeling much annoyed to see at
each try a little more of it stick out of that river, when I saw my poleman give
up the business suddenly, and stretch himself flat on the deck, without even
taking the trouble to haul his pole in. He kept hold on it though, and it trailed
in the water. At the same time, the fireman, whom I could also see below me,
sat down abruptly before his furnace and ducked his head. I was amazed.

Then I had to look at the river mighty quick, because there was a snag in the
fairway. Sticks, little sticks, were flying about—thick: they were whizzing
before my nose, dropping below me, striking behind me against my pilot-house.
All this time the river, the shore, the woods, were very quiet—perfectly quiet.
I could only hear the heavy splashing thump of the stern-wheel and the patter
of these things. We cleared the snag clumsily. Arrows, by Jove!

(pp. 74–5)

The eye is the leading sense. Conrad does not tell you things in the order they
happened (On the bank the natives began to shoot arrows . . . the poleman was
shot . . . etc.)—but in the order he saw them happen. Understanding lags
behind sight: he sees 'little sticks' first, and realizes they are arrows slightly
afterwards. It is a very dramatic extension of the technique of telling a story
from the point of view of a single character: here 'point of view' is literally right.

Earlier, I suggested that it might be illuminating to compare Conrad's technique with that of the cinema. In the passage we have just been looking at, the
sequence of shots could follow the narrative exactly. And there are other
aspects of this novel which seem to me to be cinematic—in particular the first
part of the story, where the action does not proceed in a continuous stream,
but is seen in a series of vivid, intensely visual snatches, or 'shots'.

Take, for example, the way in which the monotonous journey down the west
coast of Africa is punctuated by incidents. Or the way in which the nature of
the coastal station is realized through a selection of detailed glimpses: the

derelict machinery, the chain gang, the 'grove of death'. If anyone wanted to film *Heart of Darkness* he would find the camera-work already plotted. Even the dialogue often sounds strangely like a film-script. The film would, of course, need to be in black and white.

In this Section we have been primarily concerned with Conrad's technique. We have seen that he has some roots in the nineteenth-century tradition as well as a desire to innovate and explore. But concentration on experiment has not led to any lack of concern with the moral of the story. The didactic element of earlier novel-writing is still strongly present, and as before, it is inseparable from the way in which the story is made. But in the rules he has laid down for the telling of his story, Conrad has been more strict with himself than most of his predecessors. Having decided to write from the point of view of a man who knows he has had a rare experience, but does not understand all it has meant to him, Conrad does not cheat by taking up a more comfortable position when the going gets rough. And, having set up a powerful group of symbolic contrasts, and a limited range of colours, he sticks to them, even though it might have been easier not to. The tighter organization that we saw in Henry James appears in Conrad's novel too.

2 THEMES

ithin Marlow's story, several themes are prominent. Identify those that seem to you most important, and comment on their relation to the themes of any of the nineteenth-century novels we have studied.

I've singled out three:

1. Imperialism
2. Self-deception and self-discovery
3. Darkness, or the nature of evil.

These labels are very rough, but I hope they are accurate enough to be recognizable areas of the novel.

(i) Imperialism

I hope you will agree that neither 1 nor 3 have been prominent themes in the novels we have so far studied. (If you want to say that *Wuthering Heights* also contemplates the nature of evil, then you clearly think it is a more mystical novel than I do: but it's a work that can bear a wide variety of interpretations—and an obviously exceptional one.) So far, all the novels we have read have been more or less domesticated—even quite large portions of *Huckleberry Finn* are devoted to housekeeping. But one of the most strikingly 'new' things about *Heart of Darkness* is its setting, and its immense distance from the orthodoxies of Western society and family life.

However, it's not quite fair to say that an exotic setting was entirely new. It may well owe something to a very respectable but popular tradition of adventure stories. Re-read the description of the 'wild and gorgeous' native woman on pages 102–3.

Do you catch a faint scent of Rider Haggard? (*King Solomon's Mines* was published in 1886, *She* in 1887.) At first it may seem rather surprising that novelists made no more out of the building of the Empire. But on the whole the English novel of the nineteenth-century did not concern itself with the adventures that might befall the few, but with problems that could find reflection in the lives of many. In any case, imperialism was not a very prominent issue in England until fairly late: empire-fever did not set in until after Victoria was declared Empress of India in 1876.

Re-read the first part of *Heart of Darkness*, up to the bottom of page 9 ('and offer a sacrifice to . . .'). What is the point of Conrad's lengthy description of the river's ancient glories, and what is the purpose of Marlow's ironies?

Conrad's (or perhaps his narrator's) sentiments are the orthodox pieties of British imperialism. It's romantic, stirring stuff, to be taken with a pinch of salt perhaps:

Hunters for gold or pursuers of fame, they all had gone out on that stream, bearing the sword, and often the torch, messengers of the might within the land, bearers of a spark from the sacred fire.

(pp. 5–6)

Notice that the sword comes before the torch! Marlow challenges the complacency of this attitude with his reminder that to the Romans the Thames Valley was once the equivalent of the 'white man's burden', even 'the white man's grave': once we were the barbarians. Look particularly carefully at page 9: does the irony persist here, or does Marlow genuinely believe that 'we' are better than 'they' were?

I think he does—but he means only the British. What he describes as the Roman administration here is what he witnessed in the Congo, under Belgian government. Conrad was an enthusiastic, not very critical patriot of his adopted country. He genuinely believed that British imperialism was redeemed by an 'idea'—for which you might substitute the word 'principle'. His reference to the 'vast amount of red' on the map (p. 14) is also, I am sure, quite without irony. Nevertheless, though the anonymity of the territory Marlow went to does not make it a type of every colonial administration, it is a solemn warning of what might happen to a country governed without an 'idea'.

As I've already suggested, Marlow sets off as a kind of blank, and is practically motiveless: what takes him to the Congo is a mixture of idle curiosity and the need for a job. He is as unprejudiced as it is possible to be and this lends conviction to the attack on colonialism. I don't think it is necessary for us here to study this attack in much detail. If you are in any doubt about the strength of Conrad's feeling, re-read on to the top of page 31 ('the grove of death'). In any case, try to isolate some of those aspects of the colonial situation which Conrad particularly emphasizes.

The first thing that strikes me is the futility and the utter trivialization which in this situation has become a major crime. This is clear from Marlow's account of his predecessor's death (p. 13): Fresleven had quarrelled with a native chief over two black hens—and this trivial cause leads to his own death and (apparently) the destruction of the whole village community. It especially stands out in his description of the voyage down the west coast of Africa.

African boat flying Belgian flag crossing Stanley Rapids, Congo River (Mansell Collection)

Now and then a boat from the shore gave one a momentary contact with reality. It was paddled by black fellows. You could see from afar the white of their eyeballs glistening. They shouted, sang; their bodies streamed with perspiration; they had faces like grotesque masks—these chaps; but they had bone, muscle, a wild vitality, an intense energy of movement, that was as natural and true as the surf along their coast. They wanted no excuse for being there. They were a great comfort to look at. For a time I would feel I belonged still to a world of straightforward facts; but the feeling would not last long. Something would turn up to scare it away. Once, I remember, we came upon a man-of-war anchored off the coast. There wasn't even a shed there, and she was shelling the bush. It appears the French had one of their wars going on thereabouts. Her ensign dropped limp like a rag; the muzzles of the long six-inch guns stuck out all over the low hull; the greasy, slimy swell swung her up lazily and let her down, swaying her thin masts. In the empty immensity of earth, sky and water, there she was, incomprehensible, firing into a continent. . . .

(p. 21)

We are used to the idea that a novel should provide a moral lesson—even a kind of sermon. But have we met a challenge to the conscience of Western society on quite this world-scale before?

Perhaps Marlow's journey from innocence to experience reflects the degradation of the imperialist ideal: at first an adventure, then a racket, then a crime, and at last revealing itself as an intolerable evil. But was there ever an imperia-list ideal worth the name—even the British 'idea'? Conrad draws a continuous contrast between the high-sounding theories (or 'ideas') of those who stay at home, and the vileness of those who do the actual 'administration'. The effects of a bad colonial policy are expressed most clearly in the few paragraphs describing Marlow's first sight of the utter dereliction of the station at the foot of the rapids (pp. 23–8). The material benefits that colonization was supposed to bring lie broken and useless, and the people too are no more than broken-down machinery. The whole land has been made hideous, and its natives are subject to a foreign code they cannot understand. The men on the chain-gang 'were called criminals, and the outraged law, like the bursting shells, had come to them, an insoluble mystery from the sea' (p. 25). The dying men in the 'grove of death' were 'Brought from all the recesses of the coast in all the legality of time contracts' (p. 26) but the law was not theirs. They were subject not because they were inferior, but because of an 'accident' (page 9): the superior arma-ments of another race. Conrad had no sympathy with racialist theories. He did not believe in the inherent superiority of any one race over another, nor in the right of one nation to subjugate another by force. But he also isolated more subtle degradations: look at the description of the native fireman on page 61. I think you may find its tone rather shocking, but just why does Conrad say 'A few months of training had done for that really fine chap'? Or look at his account of the 'restraint' of the hungry cannibals (p. 69): 'equal' does not mean 'the same' to Conrad: as he sees it, tradition plays far too large a part in the formation of the individuals of different nations for that. There *are* many moments when Conrad does not seem entirely free of racial prejudices: (what for example, do you make of his attitude to the Manager's 'boy' on p. 35?) but we are talking about developments in the novel, rather than the short-comings of particular novelists. In what previous novels on this Course have the differences between nations and races figured at all?

In *Huckleberry Finn*, of course, then in *On the Eve, Cousin Bette, Anna Karenina* (mostly implied in the debate about 'Russianness') but in the English novels hardly at all. Now, in *Heart of Darkness* we find a theme that is international, even inter-racial, with a world-wide importance. Conrad's novel is far more cosmopolitan than any we have so far studied. Conrad uses irony to make this enormous and shocking subject manageable. His feelings about it are very powerful and without some sort of control they might have taken over the story. Indeed, when you began this novel, you could have been forgiven for thinking that it would be entirely a satirical attack on imperialism: there are touches of the macabre in Marlow's preparations for departure; ironic bitter-ness in the description of the voyage; a further ironic technique at work in the way the characters at the lower stations are summed up. But although irony makes this theme prominent, it also prevents rage and compassion from getting out of hand and taking over the story. Gradually other themes emerge and gain prominence.

(ii) Self-deception and self-discovery

With this theme we are back on very familiar ground. Is there a single one of our nineteenth-century novels where this is not an issue? And if there are no exceptions, does it mean that this is not an issue at all, but a meaningless formula that can cover almost any human situation?

❂❂❂❂❂❂❂❂❂❂❂❂❂❂❂❂❂❂❂❂❂❂❂❂❂❂❂❂❂❂

I think I want to make two exceptions: the characters of *Cousin Bette* seem to know pretty well everything there is to know about themselves; nor is her own nature one of the things that Maisie discovers. So although I agree that the formula can cover an enormous variety of situations I don't think it is meaningless to say that it is one of the major preoccupations of the nineteenth-century novel. Self-consciousness as a subject, and the use of a first person narrator or concentration on the point of view of a single character as a technique are clearly related.

Marlow's self-discovery depends on Kurtz. His self-deception is quite involuntary—as I said before, he goes to the Congo entirely free from prejudices. He gets hold of the idea that Kurtz is a great man with lofty philanthropic ideals, quite different from everyone else he encounters. Eventually he discovers that the ideals have given way to barbaric cruelty, and that Kurtz was more positively wicked than the Company's other employees; and he discovers too that although he condemns what Kurtz has done, something in him responds to this brutality, whereas he can only despise the rest. If you do not feel perfectly satisfied that this is a reasonable outline of what happens, read again the part of the novel from the time Marlow first hears Kurtz's name (p. 29) to the time he leaves to go up-river to Kurtz's station (p. 55), and make notes on how and how much Marlow learns about Kurtz. If you are happy with this outline (or have a better account of the story) do not bother to write answers to the exercises.

❂❂❂❂❂❂❂❂❂❂❂❂❂❂❂❂❂❂❂❂❂❂❂❂❂❂❂❂❂❂

No one is very explicit; everyone is guarded, envious. Kurtz appears to be very successful; he sends down large quantities of ivory and is in line for promotion. He is favoured by the Company's chiefs in Europe (p. 30). Apparently he first becomes a mystery to Marlow in a very prosaic way: the Manager speaks of him, and the Manager turns everything into a mystery: his smile 'came at the end of his speeches to make the meaning of the commonest phrase appear absolutely inscrutable'. In this case, mystery remains appropriate: Marlow sees Kurtz's painting:

Then I noticed a small sketch in oils, on a panel, representing a woman, draped and blindfolded, carrying a lighted torch. The background was sombre— almost black. The movement of the woman was stately, and the effect on the face was sinister.

(p. 40)

A strange thing to find in such a place, and deeply enigmatic: what do you think it means to Marlow? It is immediately after this that Marlow is given his fullest account of Kurtz so far (p. 41). But something about this paragraph is even more significant than the account of Kurtz's remarkable qualities: what?

❂❂❂❂❂❂❂❂❂❂❂❂❂❂❂❂❂❂❂❂❂❂❂❂❂❂❂❂❂❂

Kurtz and Marlow are bracketed together; even better they are both made out to be 'of the new gang—the gang of virtue'. Marlow is amused, but subconsciously, isn't he flattered, too? After all, his own fierce reactions have already marked him off in his own eyes from the colonists he has so far met. This is almost confirmation from another source that he really is better than those around him.

And what about the ever-increasing compulsion Marlow feels to meet Kurtz? Look especially at the last paragraph of the first section (p. 51):

I wasn't very interested in him. No. Still, I was curious to see whether this man, who had come out equipped with moral ideas of some sort, would climb to the top after all and how he would set about his work when there.

Does that 'No' convince you that Marlow really was not very interested in Kurtz? Marlow came out with no particular moral ideas, but in the face of experience he has acquired them. And the primeval forest, in which Kurtz is hidden, holds for Marlow both 'menace', and 'appeal' (p. 43).

The Manager hates Kurtz, who therefore seems to represent the opposite of the greed and incompetence that so enrage Marlow. Kurtz shuns the station, and Marlow sees him as 'Perhaps . . . just simply a fine fellow who stuck to his work for its own sake' (p. 53). (In other words, Kurtz is practically an Englishman—remember what the red on the map means to Marlow.)

The Manager quotes Kurtz: 'Each station should be like a beacon on the road towards better things, a centre for trade, of course, but also for humanizing, improving, instructing'—and calls him an ass for such sentiments. Marlow's reaction is plain: 'I could have spat upon their hats' (p. 54). The evidence for Kurtz's greatness is fragmentary, and Marlow bases his feelings on conjecture, on his antagonism towards the *status quo*, and on the identification that has been accidently established between them. When at last he is ready to go up river he says 'I was then rather excited at the prospect of meeting Kurtz very soon' (p. 55)·—surely an understatement.

I want to raise only a few points about Part II here, and return to it for another purpose in my next section. So if you feel that this would be a good point to re-read Part II, you can save yourself time by also assembling notes on what Marlow makes of the jungle and its 'mystery', which we will have to raise here,

Early morning on the Congo River, Stanleyville—now Kisangani (Mansell Collection)

but will also return to later. In any case, make notes on what more Marlow (and the reader) learns about Kurtz before he actually reaches his station.

I asked you what you thought Kurtz's painting meant to Marlow: you may have felt a bit embarrassed by it—it seems such an obvious piece of symbolism, a light shining into darkness. It's the same light as the beacon, in the words the Manager quotes (p. 54). To Marlow, Kurtz is an invisible point of light, hidden in the unfathomable darkness of the forest, the opposite of the moral blackness which hangs around the Company's other employers. (Did you notice how many of the incidents that take place while Marlow is waiting for his rivets happen *at night*?) So far, Conrad has been mainly concerned to identify the moral darkness; in the second part he turns his attention more towards the darkness of the forest, at once more real, and more metaphysical. But the elements are really inseparable.

The journey up-river is exciting and dangerous: for Marlow 'it crawled towards Kurtz—exclusively'. But there are other excitements, which at this stage do not seem to be connected with Kurtz the torch-bearer at all. The native life Marlow glimpses on the banks of the great river is incomprehensible:

The prehistoric man was cursing us, praying to us, welcoming us—who could tell? We were cut off from the comprehension of our surroundings; we glided past like phantoms, wondering and secretly appalled, as sane men would be before an enthusiastic outbreak in a madhouse. We could not understand because we were too far and could not remember because we were travelling in the night of first ages, of those ages that are gone, leaving hardly a sign—and no memories.

(p. 59)

But if the forest holds menace, it also has an appeal, for those who can respond to it:

It was unearthly, and the men were—No, they were not inhuman. Well, you know, that was the worst of it—this suspicion of their not being inhuman. It would come slowly to one. They howled and leaped, and spun, and made horrid faces; but what thrilled you was just the thought of their humanity—like yours—the thought of your remote kinship with this wild and passionate uproar. Ugly. Yes, it was ugly enough; but if you were man enough you would admit to yourself that there was in you just the faintest trace of a response to the terrible frankness of that noise, a dim suspicion of there being a meaning in it which you—you so remote from the night of first ages—could comprehend.

(pp. 59–60)

I called this section *Self-deception and self-discovery*. But is this accurate? Does not Marlow's recognition of the wilderness's appeal rather suggest that his eyes are fully open to his sub-conscious impulses, and that there is no self-deception involved?

The point is that he has no idea of what it would mean to follow these impulses. He only finds out when he discovers the truth about Kurtz, and then he is utterly horrified, and suffers some kind of mental and spiritual, as well as physical, crisis.

Meanwhile, his eagerness to meet Kurtz is growing stronger—so strong that he almost forgets the ambiguous warning to 'Approach cautiously'. (The earlier part of the message—'Hurry up'—speaks more strongly to him.) But he is also growing more critical: 'The approach to this Kurtz grubbing for ivory in the wretched bush was beset by as many dangers as though he had been an enchanted princess sleeping in a fabulous castle.' *This Kurtz* and *grubbing* suggest bad-tempered impatience, but the simile is highly significant. It suggests how very important it is to Marlow to reach Kurtz's castle. Perhaps the bad temper is a product of his impatience, caused by the delaying fog. (The fog is a symbolic barrier as well as a real one; another darkness, or a moat around the castle.) It could be that Kurtz is an even more ruthless exploiter of the wilderness than those at the lower stations. Look at Marlow's fullest account of what he expected to find, on pages 78–9. It comes at the moment he realizes Kurtz is probably dead: Kurtz might have been worse, but he might have been so much a better man than the whites Marlow has so far encountered.

Conrad takes great pains to keep us aware of the speaking voice of Marlow. At this point his speech breaks, he asks for tobacco. His tone is irascible, and the course of his narrative, which has so far pushed up-stream, so that we know no more than Marlow at any point in his journey, suddenly breaks dramatically, and falls into anger and confusion. At the top of page 81 you may well have felt yourself completely lost. Who is this girl, suddenly appearing? And the lie? We've heard of Marlow's almost physical loathing of untruth before (p. 44). If you did feel suddenly lost, did you think it was because of a patch of bad writing, or because you weren't clever enough to cope—or what?

A solution that exonerates both sides (and I think it is the correct one) is that this sudden patch of confusion is deliberate. We have followed Marlow's mental voyage of discovery. We've seen him get impatient and fretful as he gets nearer his goal. Now he makes a kind of rush at the truth, attacking it wildly. But it resists his muddled, unco-ordinated attack, and so he retires, recoups his strength, and then moves in again more slowly.

Congo river steamer (Radio Times Hulton Picture Library)

For the moment, however, his discourse becomes furious, irrational, and almost comically macabre. Look at the virtually insane way his speech moves in this paragraph:

And the lofty frontal bone of Mr Kurtz! They say the hair goes on growing sometimes, but this—ah—specimen, was impressively bald. The wilderness had patted him on the head, and, behold, it was like a ball—an ivory ball; it had caressed him, and—lo!—he had withered; it had taken him, loved him, embraced him, got into his veins, consumed his flesh, and sealed his soul to its own by the inconceivable ceremonies of some devilish initiation. He was its spoiled and pampered favourite. Ivory? I should think so. Heaps of it, stacks of it. . . .

(p. 81)

Is this the reaction of someone disappointed in a man about whom he was only curious? The discovery of how Kurtz got his ivory is a terrible shock to Marlow; indeed, it almost kills him. It is such a shock because Marlow has discovered how much closer he is to the abominations of Kurtz than the wretched mediocrities of the other traders.

We have already discussed the cinematic technique of this novel. Marlow first discovers for certain that the truth is horrible through his eyes. When he first sees the Inner Station it looks ordinary enough; but when he examines it through binoculars (another symbolic touch) he learns that what he thought were ornamental knobs on the posts of a broken fence, are in fact human heads.

We are now into Part III, where Marlow acknowledges his identification with Kurtz. I don't think I need to take you through this in detail, but I should like you to consider the following extracts in their context, and try to establish their significance for your own satisfaction. In certain cases, I have added a brief question to direct you towards what I think is the point.

p. 92   'I went a little farther,' he said, 'then still a little farther—till I had gone so far that I don't know how I'll ever get back.'

What was the Russian sailor going into? And what implications does this have for Marlow?

p. 98   But the wilderness had found him out early, and had taken on him a terrible vengeance for the fantastic invasion. I think it had whispered to him things about himself which he did not know, things of which he had no conception till he took counsel with this great solitude—and the whisper had proved irresistibly fascinating.

Had the wilderness told Marlow anything about himself which he did not previously know?

p. 99   The young man looked at me with surprise. I suppose it did not occur to him that Mr Kurtz was no idol of mine.

p. 102   He rustled one of the letters, and looking straight in my face said, 'I am glad'. Somebody had been writing to him about me. These special recommendations were turning up again.

p. 105   . . . I found myself lumped along with Kurtz as a partisan of methods for which the time was not ripe: I was unsound! Ah! but it was something to have at least a choice of nightmares.

26

What is the choice of nightmares?

p. 109 I did not betray Mr Kurtz—it was ordered I should never betray him—
it was written I should be loyal to the nightmare of my choice. I was
anxious to deal with this shadow by myself alone—and to this day I
don't know why I was so jealous of sharing with anyone the peculiar
blackness of that experience.

What do you make of the words 'ordered' and 'written'?

p. 110 And I remember I confounded the beat of the drum with the beating
of my heart, and was pleased at its calm regularity.

p. 113 But his soul was mad. . . . I had—for my sins, I suppose—to go through
the ordeal of looking into it myself.

p. 115 I was, so to speak, numbered with the dead. It is strange how I accepted
this unforeseen partnership, this choice of nightmares forced upon me
in the tenebrous land invaded by these mean and greedy phantoms.

p. 120 It is his extremity that I seem to have lived through.

I could have noted (perhaps you have) several more references to the strange
bond between Kurtz and Marlow. Two general points can be made about
these extracts. First, the 'unforeseen partnership' (p. 115) was unrecognized
before Marlow learnt how Kurtz got his ivory, though the factors that made it
were evident: the shock made Marlow acknowledge his kinship. Second, you
must be aware that Conrad makes his way through his extremely complex
narrative with great care and precision.

I said at the beginning of this section that self-discovery was a common theme
in a large number of nineteenth-century novels. That is not what is new to
Heart of Darkness. What *is* new here is just what Marlow discovers in himself.
No one in any of the earlier novels we have studied secretly hankered after a
malevolent godhead. I've suggested before that it is useful to remember that
Conrad's writing is contemporaneous with the early development of psycho-
analysis and investigation of the subconscious. What Freud found there was
deeply shocking to many people. What Conrad found in his researches must
have been equally startling.

But what about the last scene of Marlow's narrative—his meeting with the
Intended? If you're very pressed for time you can skip this bit, but I can't
resist it.

There's nothing that would startle the conventional consciousness here. Go
through it and make a note of some of its most glaring clichés.

Isn't the whole scene rather a cliché? But used with a high degree of irony:

'He was a remarkable man,' I said, unsteadily. Then before the appealing
fixity of her gaze, that seemed to watch for more words on my lips, I went on,
'It was impossible not to—'

'Love him,' she finished eagerly, silencing me into an appalled dumbness.

(p. 127)

27

Poor Marlow, who came to some sort of terms with Kurtz, finds it impossible to come to any sort of terms with Kurtz's Intended—except by telling lies. He has a very Victorian notion of women (there's a dreadful passage on page 19, and another on page 81) and really the would-have-been Mrs Kurtz does nothing to dispel it. The drawing-room pieties she and Marlow exchange make a staggering contrast with the rest of the novel. I'm sure they were meant to, and that the scene was meant to be partially comic. After all, we've noticed a vein of rather black comedy throughout. But for Marlow the scene is embarrassment stretched to the point of agony, and he gets out of it with another cliché: 'The last word he pronounced was—your name.' But it's also the thing Marlow hates most: a lie. The part of him that hates lying is the part he likes to acknowledge. The part of him that tells the lie is not just trying to get out of an awkward social situation: it's also the hidden part, that owes its allegiance to Kurtz and the darkness.

Note

[Later, if you have time, I suggest you read the much shorter story, *The Secret Sharer* in the same volume as *Heart of Darkness*. It's much simpler than our novel, but it has in common with it the theme of an obscure bond, established between two strangers.]

(iii) Darkness

I admit I'm not very sure what to call this section: 'darkness' obviously needs inverted commas, because it is a metaphor for some kind of moral quality. The nature of evil—or something? I'm not sure that 'something' would not be the best title, because it's very difficult to understand what Conrad's darkness is, but think about evil for a moment: is that what Marlow comes to face? Look carefully at the kind of vocabulary he uses.

Conrad uses words like 'evil', 'devil', and phrases like 'powers of darkness' very often. I've selected only a very small proportion, and you will probably have other examples.

Evil is associated with the unexplored forest:

I saw him extend his short flipper of an arm for a gesture that took in the forest, the creek, the mud, the river—seemed to beckon with a dishonouring flourish before the sunlit face of the land a treacherous appeal to *the lurking death, to the hidden evil, to the profound darkness of its heart.*

p. 54 (my italics)

It's rather an awkward sentence, but concentrate on the three phrases in italics. Conrad seems to treat them as equally applicable to the forest, which was indeed dark and dangerous—but evil? In what sense can a jungle be evil?

Surely only by association—but that is not what Conrad implies. Elsewhere he suggests that the wilderness might be truth:

. . . the silent wilderness surrounding this cleared speck on the earth struck me as something great and invincible, *like evil or truth*, waiting patiently for the passing away of this fantastic invasion.

It's a phrase meant to be profoundly meaningful, but in effect it is more impressive than significant. Meaning is hard to find: there is evil in the forest, certainly; and Marlow discovers some kind of truth about his own nature. But Conrad applies these terms to the forest itself and implies that they are not opposites, though the 'civilized' world might like to think they are. He postulates some kind of unattached evil, independent of the malevolent activities of men. Such a thing may or may not exist: Conrad is perfectly entitled to claim that it does. But *in this story* does it exist anywhere outside the use of words like 'evil', and 'darkness'? There are evil men and evil deeds, in varying degrees of solidity. But do you have any sense of the presence of the abstract evil that Conrad claims hangs over the scene? Think about it for a moment: I'll be returning to it later.

Conrad says that the forest offers alternatives of truth and evil, but I'm sure you are right if you felt that truth (or light) is not much more than a foil to show up the darkness—or evil. Perhaps you have noticed that I have been using 'darkness' and 'evil' as if they were alternatives. Normally, this would be a completely improper usage. Is there any justification for it here?

I hope you noticed that Conrad chose words relating to real and metaphorical darkness not just with reference to the forest and the obscure wickednesses of Kurtz. I've selected a handful of examples from the early part of the story, but you could have found many others:

p. 33 . . . the first glance at the place was enough to let you see the flabby devil was running that show.

p. 41 'He is an emissary of pity and science and progress, and devil knows what else.'

p. 69 Why in the name of all the roaring devils of hunger they didn't go for us—they were thirty to five—and have a good tuck-in for once, amazes me now when I think of it.

Obstensibly, of course, such usages are colloquial. But in this context they acquire a new weight—if not necessarily a new meaning. They function ironically, and unite the comic with the deadly serious as a macabre reminder that there is an infinite variety of devils:

p. 61 . . . he had filed teeth, too, the poor devil, and the wool of his pate shaved into queer patterns, and three ornamental scars on each of his cheeks. He ought to have been clapping his hands and stamping his feet on the bank, instead of which he was hard at work, a thrall to strange witchcraft, full of improving knowledge. He was useful because he had been instructed; and what he knew was this—that should the water in that transparent thing disappear, the evil spirit inside the boiler would get angry through the greatness of his thirst, and take a terrible vengeance.[1]

---

[1] Dennis Johnson comments: 'It is interesting that the native, in spite of his "instruction" should interpret the boiler in terms of the forest—just as the white man, in spite of his knowledge, tends to interpret the forest, one might say, in terms of the boiler.'

But these are insignificant demons compared with the two giants: the devil of the white-man's stupidity:

I've seen the devil of violence, and the devil of greed, and the devil of hot desire; but, by all the stars! these were strong, lusty, red-eyed devils, that swayed and drove men—men, I tell you. But as I stood on this hillside, I foresaw that in the blinding sunshine of that land I would become acquainted with a flabby, pretending, weak-eyed devil of a rapacious and pitiless folly.

(p. 25)

—and the devil hidden in the forest: these, I think, represent Marlow's 'choice of nightmares'.

Very much more could be said about evil and darkness in this novel, but I want to limit myself to two points. First, consider this passage from *The Great Tradition*:

Is anything added to the oppressive mysteriousness of the Congo by such sentences as: It was the stillness of an implacable force brooding over an inscrutable intention—?[1] The same vocabulary, the same adjectival insistence upon inexpressible and incomprehensible mystery, is applied to the evocation of human profundities and spiritual horrors; to magnifying a thrilled sense of the unspeakable potentialities of the human soul. The actual effect is not to magnify but rather to muffle . . . we have an adjectival and worse than supererogatory insistence on 'unspeakable rites', 'unspeakable secrets', 'monstrous passions', 'inconceivable mystery' and so on.[2]

Leavis then quotes the passage that in your edition appears on pages 112–13 ('I tried to break the spell . . . struggling blindly with itself'). Do you agree with him that the 'cheapening' (which this sort of vocabulary produces) 'is little short of disastrous'? Perhaps you noticed that Leavis himself used 'inexpressible', 'incomprehensible' and 'unspeakable': do you think it was with any sense of irony?

I certainly agree with Leavis up to a point, and I expect you found that Conrad's emphasis on the mystery led you to feel not awe, but bafflement—and even irritation. There are magnificent passages in this story which seem more than adequately to call up the mystery of the wilderness: look for example at page 58:

The word ivory would ring in the air for a while—and on we went again into the silence, along empty reaches, round the still bends, between the high walls of our winding way. . . .

That communicates something solid; but this simply obfuscates:

He was alone, and I before him did not know whether I stood on the ground or floated in the air. I've been telling you what we said—repeating the phrases we pronounced—but what's the good? They were common everyday words—

[1] Your edition, page 56.
[2] F. R. Leavis: *The Great Tradition* Penguin Books, 1962.

the familiar, vague sounds exchanged on every waking day of life. But what of that? They had behind them, to my mind, the terrific suggestiveness of words heard in dreams, of phrases spoken in nightmares. Soul! If anybody ever struggled with a soul, I am the man.

(p. 112)

The worst of it is, that this kind of thing is infectious. It spreads through the whole fabric of the story, so that we read all of it looking for 'the terrific sugges-tiveness of words heard in dreams'; trying to find even more meaning than is obviously present. It makes it difficult to take a sentence like this literally: 'He had taken a high seat amongst the devils of the land—I mean literally' (p. 82). And that despite Conrad's insistence that we should take the sentence as an unmetaphorical statement of fact.

What, after all, is the mystery? We know a great deal about Kurtz's practices: he set himself up as a god in a barbaric religion, and killed large numbers to maintain his power—and get his ivory; there are suggestions of human sacrifice and cannibalism, and it is suggested that he took a native mistress—a very Victorian 'horror' that. Is the mystery then that he did deeds even nastier than these? Or is the mystery not what he did, but *why* he did it? Again, if you look carefully, you can find ample evidence of possible motivations and opportuni-ties. I think the real problem is, just what is it that is so mysterious? Or, to put it much more crudely, what is all the fuss about?

Of course, you may well not agree. You may think that what is at work is a kind of self-imposed censorship: Conrad does not want to shock his readers. But if this is the case, he would be protecting only the most superficial reader, incapable of being shocked by the horrors of oppression, or by the fact that a white man should 'turn native' in the most barbarian way, yet sensitive to specific details of primitive rituals.

Another partial explanation might be that Conrad was simply following one of the traditions common to thrillers and ghost stories: using words like 'inscrut-able', 'incomprehensible' and so on as an extreme form of emphasis, trying to suggest horrors beyond anything that even the most stretched imagination could produce.

Partly, I think, because of their curiously infectious nature, it's easy to place too great an emphasis on such abstruse passages. When we read the novel carefully, there is actually little that is beyond comprehension—and what there is, is surely not enough to obscure the merits of the whole. Yet I think there is a fault here: perhaps it is simply redundancy. The novel would surely be no poorer without a sentence like 'it was the stillness of an implacable force brood-ing over an inscrutable intention'.

This is possibly the most problematical area of a difficult novel. Can you see any ways in which it might be connected with the nineteenth-century novel, or any new directions in which it might be pointing?

It's difficult to find any similarities. On the whole, nineteenth-century novelists concerned themselves only with what they could describe satisfactorily. Any-thing that was impossible, vague, nebulous, imprecise or indefinable had no place. In a sense, a novel was its author's definition of his vision of society. But although you might say that this kind of definition forms part of *Heart of Darkness* (it's especially strong in the early stages) it clearly accounts for nothing like the whole. Conrad deliberately chose to write about a man who experienced something he did not understand; nor did he supplement Marlow's account with an authorial interpretation which would tell his readers how he expected them to understand the story. *Marlow* is clearly not happy to work in obscurities: the sense of someone trying to make sense of or define his experience is very strong. But *Conrad* does not intervene as an interpreter of Marlow's story because it will not reach an acceptable easy level of definition: and I think most of his predecessors would have done—except, possibly, in their ghost-stories, a form most of the great nineteenth-century novelists tried.

Look back to page 7:

'The yarns of seamen have a direct simplicity, the whole meaning of which lies within the shell of a cracked nut. But Marlow was not typical (if his propensity to spin yarns be excepted), and to him the meaning of an episode was not inside like a kernel but outside, enveloping the tale which brought it out only as a glow brings out a haze, in the likeness of one of those misty halos that sometimes are made visible by the spectral illumination of moonshine.'

Study the metaphor vary carefully: I think—or hope—that Conrad does not mean it to be capable of a precise interpretation. Of one thing, however, I think we can be very certain: that what Conrad wanted from a novel was very different from the effect most nineteenth-century novelists expected to produce. We've come a long way from Henry James even: his demand for 'solidity of specification' was something most of the novelists we have so far studied would have agreed with. Conrad wants to present tentativeness and uncertainty. It's not that he cannot reach a point of definition: he aims beyond it, at the 'misty halo' outside the kernel. But does he leave his reader free to argue that a kernel does not really possess the aura he claims for it?

Was this, in the case of *Heart of Darkness*, a worthwhile attempt? Does this novel give us any sense of the expanding frontiers of consciousness—at least, of the novelist's consciousness? Or does it only puzzle us with no good reason? E. M. Forster suspected that Conrad was '. . , misty in the middle as well as at the edges, that the secret casket of his genius contains a vapour rather than a jewel'. And in this case at least you may feel inclined to agree. What or where is the heart in *Heart of Darkness*? In this section we have been discussing three major themes; and you will probably have noticed several more minor threads running through the whole. But how are they related? Where is the unity of *Heart of Darkness*?

What binds all the elements together is that they happened to, or were experienced by, one man: Marlow—or Conrad. It ought to be enough. But I think most readers of *Heart of Darkness* would agree that the best things about the story (and they are superb) are not those that Marlow seems to consider most important. The best things may be the most old-fashioned: the scenes which so vividly condemn the degraded imperial ideals are as much defined, as solidly specified, as any nineteenth-century novelist could possibly wish. But the farther we move from this theme, the less satisfying I, at least, find this novel. The narrator (p. 10) says (perhaps a little ironically) '. . . we knew we were fated, before the ebb began to run, to hear one of Marlow's inconclusive experiences'. The inconclusiveness was certainly deliberate, but I'm not sure that it is satisfying—but then, have we any right to expect to feel at the end of a novel as if we have just enjoyed a good meal? E. M. Forster goes on to suggest that Conrad had no philosophy:

No creed, in fact. Only opinions, and the right to throw them overboard when facts make them look absurd. Opinions held under the semblance of eternity, girt with the sea, crowned with stars, and therefore easily mistaken for a creed.

Consider this carefully, and then look at the last paragraph of *Heart of Darkness*.

At the beginning of this Unit I suggested that you should make a list of things that seem new about this novel. Obviously, brief headings such as those following do not tell the whole story, but you may find they make useful reminders when you read the other four short twentieth-century novels on this Course.

Heart of Darkness is:

   (i) shorter
  (ii) more problematic
 (iii) more deliberative
 (iv) more 'intense'
  (v) it sticks more closely to its self-imposed limitations
 (vi) artistically more self conscious
 (vii) more symbolic
(viii) more cosmopolitan
 (ix) more conscience-stricken (??)
  (x) more enigmatic
 (xi) more mysterious

—than most of the novels we have so far studied. Your list will not be identical, but it should have included most of these general points. I would expect you to have found a larger number of 'mores' than 'lesses', though the qualities that *Heart of Darkness* has less of than its predecessors amount to something very considerable. Briefly, what this novel does *not* have is the assumption that we all live in the same world, all think and respond in comparable ways, and hold the same standards, even if we do not keep to them.[1] Of course, this is not in any sense a real loss, but a permanent gain, one thing more the novelist could do, while he was still as free to assume a shared experience and a basic ethos as any earlier novelist had ever been. The kind of novel we have so far been reading is not dead yet. On the other hand, though *Heart of Darkness* is positively bristling with unfamiliar new emphases, is there anything that, taken by itself, is really entirely without precedent? Every revolution has long tangled roots in the situation against which it reacts, and in many ways Conrad was deeply conservative. His novels are built on the tradition they by and large reject. You will want to bear these points in mind as you read the last four novels of this Course.

[1] But what about Wemmick in *Great Expectations?*

ACKNOWLEDGEMENTS

Grateful acknowledgement is made to the following sources for illustrations used in this unit:

Mansell Collection; Radio Times Hulton Picture Library.

The Nineteenth-century Novel and its Legacy